Creative Storytelling
With Flannelboards

written by Marsha Elyn Wright

illustrated by Patty McCloskey

Grade Pre-K – First Grade

Editors: Stephanie Oberc-Garcia
           Robert Newman
Art Director: Rita Hudson
Cover Design: Joanne Caroselli
Book Design: Shelly Brown
Graphic Artist: Carol Arriola

Cover Photography by Color Inc.

J330004 Creative Storytelling With Flannelboards
All rights reserved—Printed in the U.S.A.
Copyright © 2000 Judy/Instructo
A Division of Frank Schaffer Publications, Inc.
23740 Hawthorne Blvd., Torrance, CA 90505

Table of Contents

Tips for Cutouts and Flannelboards

Use flannelboards to make story time a hands-on experience that helps young children visualize the events of the story and keep their attention focused. When young children interact with a flannelboard, their learning comes alive! These simple ideas will help you create cutouts and flannelboards for the many activities in this book.

Fabric Cutouts

Make cutouts from felt, flannel, or other fabric using your own shapes or using the easy-to-trace patterns in the back of this book. Photocopy the pattern pages you want to use, and then cut apart the patterns. Choose the color of fabric for each pattern. Secure the pattern on top of the fabric piece by pinning or taping the pattern to the fabric. Cut around the outer edge of the solid outline to create the shape. Or trace around the pattern using a black felt-tip marker to create a bold outline, and then cut out the shape. There are also manufactured felt cutouts of letters, numbers, basic geometric shapes, and other shapes available at teacher supply stores and craft stores. You can buy fabric that has a holiday- or theme-oriented pattern and make cutouts out of the fabric pictures.

Paper Cutouts

Trace stencils to make cutouts of letters, numbers, and shapes to use with a flannelboard. Use colorful calendar cutouts or cut out illustrations from coloring books and old workbooks! Just glue a piece of felt, sandpaper, or the "hooks" portion of self-sticking Velcro to the back of each cutout. The patterns in the back of this book also create sturdy paper cutouts. Before cutting the patterns apart, laminate the pages, cover them in clear self-stick paper, or photocopy them on different colors of tagboard or thick construction paper.

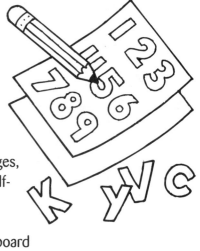

Storing Cutouts

Store your cutouts inside a resealable plastic bag. Label the bag with the name of the activity and, if appropriate, the page number where it can be found in this book. Place your storage bags in an expandable folder or box. You can also store your cutouts inside a manila folder by stapling both sides of the folder to form a large pocket. Label these folders and file them alphabetically by the title of the activity for a handy reference. You may want to use large envelopes to store your cutouts. This type of storage fits easily in filing cabinets and on shelves.

Making Flannelboards

You can purchase a manufactured flannelboard or try one of these ideas to create your own!

- **Flat Carpet Flannelboard**—Cut out a large rectangle or circle of felt or flannel. When you're doing a flannelboard activity, lay the fabric on your classroom carpet and have the children sit around it.

- **Flat Box Flannelboard**—Open and lay out flat a large cardboard box. Spray adhesive on the front. Place a large piece of felt or flannel on the front and smooth out the fabric from the center to the edges. (Attaching a thin layer of foam under the flannel works even better!) Good boxes to use include large pizza boxes, shipping boxes for large pictures, and packing boxes for posters.

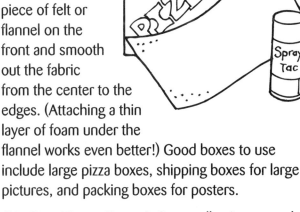

- **Big Box Flannelboard**—Spray adhesive on each side of a large box. Cut out felt or flannel pieces to match the dimensions of the sides of the box. Lay each piece on one side of the box and smooth out the fabric from the center to the edges. As you do an activity, use each side of your flannelboard box to display felt shapes.

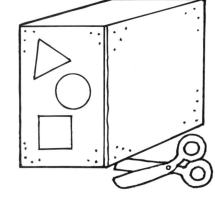

- **Small Flannelboard**—Glue a piece of felt or flannel around a small, lap-sized piece of laminate or sturdy cardboard; cover both sides. These small flannelboards make perfect lap-sized flannelboards for young children.

- **Pressboard or Foamcore Flannelboard**—Buy a large piece (at least 24" x 36") of pressboard or lightweight foamcore, either of which is available at art supply stores. Cut a length of felt or flannel that is about two inches larger on all sides than the board. Spray the front of the board with a spray adhesive. Lay the fabric on the board, leaving a two-inch overlap on all sides. Smooth out the fabric from the center to the edges. Then fold the edges back so that each corner forms a point on the back of the board. Cut off any excess fabric to leave neat corners; then use masking tape or glue to adhere the fabric to the back of the board.

- **Folding Flannelboard**—Collect two large pieces of sturdy cardboard. Cut one piece in half. Use masking tape to attach the smaller pieces to the left and right sides of the larger piece of cardboard to form two flaps. Spray adhesive on the front of the board. Lay a large piece of felt or flannel over the adhesive and smooth out the fabric from the center to the edges. Use the eraser end of a pencil to press and crease each fold so the flaps still bend. This flannelboard is perfect for displaying on a table when in use and folds up easily for quick storage.

Storytelling Secrets

There's no one way to tell stories. You simply begin. With some preparation and practice, you'll develop your own style. You'll be able to stimulate the imagination of young children as they listen to you tell stories and watch you move around cutout characters on the flannelboard. Telling stories this way can also develop the children's oral language skills and motor coordination if you give them opportunities to help tell the stories and manipulate the characters.

Establishing a Storytelling Routine

Plan a regular storytelling time at least a couple of times a week. Make this a special time by gathering the children onto a particular rug or blanket in a cozy corner of the room. Establish a routine for starting and ending your storytelling. Keep the routine simple. You might call the children to the rug for the story by ringing a bell, having a class puppet announce storytelling time, or singing a song such as the following:

"Come and Listen"
(Sung to the tune of "Are You Sleeping?")

> Come and listen, come and listen,
> To a tale, to a tale.
> Open up your ears wide,
> Sit up tall and don't hide,
> Story time, story time.

Plan how you will end storytelling time. Play marching music as a signal for the children to "march" back to their regular seats. Say a unique phrase or verse. Here are some suggestions:

So now our tale is done. Oh, wasn't it just so much fun?
Let's put a smile upon our face and tiptoe back to our own place!

Snip, snap, snout! Our tale's told out!

Now it's time to say "The End," but another tale's around the bend.

Our story time has come and gone, but the story will live on and on.

Selecting Stories

With so many stories and rhymes for children, which ones should you use with flannelboards? Choose stories and rhymes that *you* like to tell. Pick ones that have easy-to-follow plot lines and repetitive refrains so that the children can participate. Select stories and rhymes with a limited number of characters. Choose simple, appropriate ones for young children—nursery rhymes, folk tales, and fables. Pick out cumulative tales because of their repetitive pattern. Sing songs and recite poems. You can even make up your own simple story rhymes using factual information to teach the children about the life cycle of a frog!

Preparing to Tell a Story

After selecting a story, carefully read it and then put it aside. Try to think through the story until you can picture the whole sequence of events in your mind. If you stumble with parts of the story, reread the story again. Don't memorize the story. Tell it in your own words, except for specific refrains and phrases (important words in the story). Tell the story to yourself. Sometimes it helps to tell it in front of a mirror.

Decide what cutouts you need to make for the story. If backgrounds and other objects are necessary to tell the story, you need to prepare those as well as the character cutouts. Arrange the cutouts in the sequence needed to tell the story. Keep the story cutouts hidden from the audience to create excitement. One way to do this is place the cutouts and a copy of the story inside a manila folder. Staple a pocket on one side of the folder and tuck the cutouts in sequence in the pocket. Staple a copy of the story on the other side of the folder. Hold the open folder on your lap as you tell the story.

Storytelling Techniques

Storytellers often use different voices for the characters. Decide if you want to change your voice. Will a character have a high-pitched, squeaky voice or a deep, low voice? Will it talk slowly or fast? How will other characters sound? Remember, if you don't change your voice, your story will be just as exciting!

If a story is being told from a character's point of view, you might outfit yourself—nothing elaborate. Wear a shawl to tell an old woman's tale or an old straw hat for a farmer's tale.

Before you begin, place your story folder on your lap so that the cutouts are handy. Make sure you have the children's attention. As you tell the story, look at the children. When you place a cutout on the flannelboard, pause and manipulate the cutout; then turn back to the children to continue the story. Speak clearly and slowly. Pause and vary your rhythm. Let the children recite any refrains with you. If you forget part of your story, relax. The children will never know you left something out! Make your ending definite and plan a short follow-up. It could be as simple as a question: *What do you think might happen next?* Then provide a way for the children to move from the story area to the next activity.

Storytelling Tales

Anansi the Spider: A Tale From the Ashanti, Gerald McDermott (Henry Holt, 1968)

Caps for Sale, Esphyr Slobodkina (W.R. Scott, 1947)

The Gingerbread Boy, Paul Galdone (Clarion, 1979)

Henny Penny, Paul Galdone (Clarion, 1979)

The Little Old Woman Who Was Not Afraid of Anything, Linda Williams (Crowell, 1986)

Little Red Hen, Janina Domanska (Macmillan, 1973)

The Three Bears, Paul Galdone (Clarion, 1979)

The Three Billy Goats Gruff, P.C. Asbjornsen (Harcourt, 1957)

The Three Little Pigs, Paul Galdone (Clarion, 1979)

Too Much Noise, Ann McGovern (Houghton Mifflin, 1967)

Why Mosquitoes Buzz in People's Ears, Verna Aardema (Dial, 1975)

Counting Rhymes

Many counting rhymes tell stories. Children love listening to the musical language of these rhymes. The simple rhythm and repetitive phrasing make these stories easy to remember.

Five Little Monkeys

Materials: flannelboard, five monkey cutouts (pattern page 50), long fabric rectangle

Directions: Use the rectangle for the bed on the flannelboard. Add wiggly eyes and a round fabric nose to each monkey. Put the five monkey cutouts one at a time on the bed. Have the children count the cutouts from one to five. As you recite each verse, remove one monkey cutout from the bed. Repeat this story rhyme and let different children remove the cutouts from the bed.

> *Five* little monkeys jumping on the bed,
> One fell out and bumped his head.
> Mama called the doctor and the doctor said,
> "No more monkeys jumping on the bed!"

> *Four* little monkeys jumping on the bed, *(and so on)*

> *One* little monkey jumping on the bed . . .
> "No more monkeys jumping on the bed!"

Teasing Mister Alligator

Materials: flannelboard, five monkey cutouts (pattern page 50), alligator cutout (pattern page 50), fabric tree

Directions: Make a fabric tree by cutting out a large puffy cloud shape from green fabric and a narrow rectangle from brown fabric. Add wiggly eyes and fabric noses to the monkeys and alligator. Place one monkey cutout at a time on the tree. Have the children count the monkeys from one to five. Place the alligator on the flannelboard. As you recite each verse, remove one monkey from the tree. Repeat this story rhyme and let different children remove the monkeys.

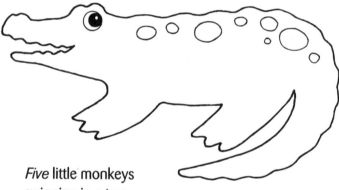

> *Five* little monkeys
> swinging in a tree,
> teasing mister alligator,

> "You can't catch me! You can't catch me!"

> "Snap!" went the alligator, "Crack" went the tree,
> And one little monkey ran away with a "Whee!"

> *Four* little monkeys swinging in a tree,
> teasing mister alligator, *(and so on)*

> *One* little monkey swinging in a tree,
> teasing mister alligator, . . .
> And the last little monkey ran away with a "Whee!"

J330004 Creative Storytelling With Flannelboards

Ten Red Apples

Materials: flannelboard, 10 red apple cutouts (pattern page 54), fabric tree

Directions: Make a fabric apple tree by cutting out a large puffy cloud shape from green fabric and a narrow rectangle from brown fabric. Add green fabric leaves to the apples. Place one apple cutout at a time on the tree. Have the children count the apples from one to ten. As you recite each verse, remove one apple cutout from the tree and give it to a child. Repeat this story rhyme and let different children remove the apples from the tree. Have the children rub their stomachs after the last verse!

Way up high in an old apple tree,
Ten red apples smiled at me.
I shook that tree as hard as I could.
Down fell an apple. My it was good!

Way up high in an old apple tree,
Nine red apples smiled at me . . . (*and so on*)

Way up high in an old apple tree,
One red apple smiled at me.
I shook that tree as hard as I could.
Down fell the apple. My it was good!
But now I have a tummy ache . . . ooh!

Ten in a Bed

Materials: flannelboard, 10 child cutouts (pattern page 50), long fabric rectangle

Directions: Use the rectangle as the bed on the flannelboard. Add fabric-paint faces and fabric clothes to the child cutouts. Put the 10 cutouts in a row on the bed one at a time. Have the children count the cutouts from one to ten. As you recite each verse, remove one child cutout from the bed. Repeat this story and let different children remove the cutouts from the bed.

There were *ten* in the bed and the little one said,
"Roll over! Roll over!"
So they all rolled over and one fell out.
There were *nine* in the bed, (*and so on*)

There were *two* in the bed and the little one said,
"Roll over! Roll over!"
So they both rolled over and *one* fell out.
There was *one* in the bed and the little one said,
"Good night!"

Three Favorite Folk Tales

The Three Billy Goats Gruff

Materials: flannelboard, three goat cutouts and one troll cutout (pattern page 51), fabric bridge

Directions: Make a fabric bridge by cutting out a wide arch from a dark-colored piece of fabric. Add cotton beards and fabric-paint faces on the goats. Add a beard on the troll with strands of yarn. Use fabric paint to make the troll's face and other details.

Once upon a time, three billy goats Gruff lived on a hillside. They ate and ate the grass. "Our grass is almost gone," said Big Billy Goat. "We need to cross the bridge to the tall grass on the other side."

"A scary troll lives under that bridge!" whispered Middle-size Billy Goat.

"A scary troll lives under that bridge!" repeated Little Billy Goat.

"I have a plan for that troll," said Big Billy Goat and he told his brothers his plan.

Trip, trap, trip, trap. Little Billy goat came tramping over the bridge. Up jumped the troll. "Who is tramping over my bridge?" growled the troll.

"It is I, Little Billy Goat Gruff," said Little Billy Goat.

"No one tramps over my bridge!" said the troll. "I'm going to eat you!"

"Oh, please don't eat me," said Little Billy Goat. "My bigger brother is coming. Wait for him." The troll looked

up and down at Little Billy Goat, and then told him to cross the bridge. Trip, trap, trip, trap. Little Billy Goat went to the tall grass.

Trip, trap, trip, trap. Middle-size Billy Goat came tramping over the bridge. Up jumped the troll. "Who is tramping over my bridge?" growled the troll.

"It is I, Middle-size Billy Goat Gruff," said Middle-size Billy Goat.

"No one tramps over my bridge!" said the troll. "I'm going to eat you!"

"Oh, please don't eat me," said Middle-size Billy Goat. "My bigger brother is coming. Wait for him." The troll looked up and down at Middle-size Billy Goat, and then told him to cross the bridge. Trip, trap, trip, trap. Middle-size Billy Goat went to the tall grass.

Trip, trap, trip, trap. Big Billy Goat came tramping over the bridge. Up jumped the troll. "Who is tramping over my bridge?" growled the troll. Big Billy Goat grunted loudly. "Yeow!" shouted the troll and he ran off the bridge. Trip, trap, trip, trap. Big Billy Goat went to the tall grass where he and his brothers live even now. And what happened to the troll? Well, no one has seen the troll since that day!

The Three Bears

Materials: flannelboard, one small bear cutout and two big bear cutouts (pattern page 52), child cutout (pattern page 50), three fabric rectangles of varying sizes, three fabric bowl-shapes of varying sizes, one small chair cutout and two big chair cutouts (pattern page 52)

Directions: Add strands of yellow-yarn hair, a fabric-paint face, and fabric clothes to make the child cutout into Goldilocks. Add fabric-paint faces on the bears. Use the rectangles for the bears' beds. Trim or reduce one big chair cutout so that it is medium size.

Once upon a time, three bears took a walk in the woods. They left three bowls of hot porridge in their cabin to cool. Soon a little girl named Goldilocks came knocking on the cabin door. Swish! The door opened! "Hello! Anyone home?" called Goldilocks. "Mmm, what's that wonderful smell?" she asked. Goldilocks tiptoed into the cabin and sat at the table.

"I'm so hungry," said Goldilocks. First she tried the biggest bowl of porridge. "This one's too hot." Next she tried the middle-size bowl. "This one's too cold." Then she tried the littlest bowl. "This one's just right!" She ate until she finished it!

"I'm so tired," said Goldilocks. First she tried the biggest rocking chair. "This one's too hard." Next she tried the middle-size chair. "This one's too soft." Then she tried the littlest chair. "This one's just right!" She rocked until she broke the chair!

"I'm so sleepy," said Goldilocks. First she tried the biggest bed. "This one's too high." Next she tried the middle-size bed. "This one's too low." Then she tried the littlest bed. "This one's just right!" She rested until she fell asleep!

When the three bears came home, they found the door open. "Someone's been eating my porridge," said Papa Bear.

"Someone's been eating my porridge," said Mama Bear.

"Someone's been eating *my* porridge," said Baby Bear, "and it's all gone!"

"Someone's been sitting in my chair," said Papa Bear.

"Someone's been sitting in my chair," said Mama Bear.

"Someone's been sitting in *my* chair," said Baby Bear, "and it's all broken!"

The three bears went upstairs to their bedroom. "Someone's been sleeping in my bed," said Papa Bear.

"Someone's been sleeping in my bed," said Mama Bear.

"Someone's been sleeping in *my* bed," said Baby Bear, "and here she is!"

Suddenly, Goldilocks woke up! Her eyes grew wide when she saw the bears! "Eek! Bears!" shouted Goldilocks. Then she ran down the steps, ran through the woods, and ran all the way home!

Mama Bear and Papa Bear made more porridge and the three bears sat down to a wonderful meal. "Who was that girl?" asked Baby Bear. Mama Bear and Papa Bear just shook their heads and laughed.

The Three Little Pigs

Materials: flannelboard, three pig cutouts and one wolf cutout (pattern page 53), three child cutouts (pattern page 50), four strips of yellow fabric, six strips of brown fabric, red fabric rectangle and triangle

Directions: Add fabric-paint faces on the pigs and wolf. Use the yellow strips for the house of straw, the brown strips for the house of sticks, and the rectangle and triangle for the house of bricks.

Once upon a time, three little pigs set off to seek their fortune. The first little pig met a man selling straw. "Please, Sir, sell me your straw so I can build a house." So the man sold him the straw and the first little pig built a straw house.

The second little pig met a man selling sticks. "Please, Sir, sell me your sticks so I can build a house." So the man sold him the sticks and the second little pig built a stick house.

The third little pig met a man selling bricks. "Please, Sir, sell me your bricks so I can build a house." So the man sold him the bricks and the third little pig built a brick house.

Soon after the little pigs built their houses, a big hungry wolf knocked on the first little pig's door. "Little pig, little pig, let me in!" growled the wolf.

"No, no, you'll never come in! Not by the hair on my chinny, chin, chin!" cried the pig.

"Then I'll huff and I'll puff and I'll blow your house in!" growled the wolf. So he huffed and he puffed and he blew the house in! The first little pig ran away as fast as he could to the second little pig.

Before long the big hungry wolf knocked on the second little pig's door. "Little pig, little pig, let me in!" growled the wolf.

"No, no, you'll never come in! Not by the hair on my chinny, chin, chin!" cried the pig.

"Then I'll huff and I'll puff and I'll blow your house in!" growled the wolf. So he huffed and he puffed and he blew the house in! The two little pigs ran away as fast as they could to the third little pig.

Before long the big hungry wolf knocked on the third little pig's door. "Little pig, little pig, let me in!" growled the wolf.

"No, no, you'll never come in! Not by the hair on my chinny, chin, chin!" cried the pig.

"Then I'll huff and I'll puff and I'll blow your house in!" growled the wolf. So he huffed and he puffed. And he huffed and he puffed. But he couldn't blow the house in! This made the wolf angry. He climbed on the roof and slid down the chimney. But the pigs were boiling soup in a big pot over a big fire. When the wolf slid down the chimney, he fell straight into the pot! "Yeow!" shouted the wolf as he raced up the chimney as fast as he could to get away from the three little pigs.

That night the three little pigs had wonderful hot soup for dinner in the brick house where they live even now. And what happened to the wolf? Well, no one has seen the wolf since that day!

Fable Fun

Use a flannelboard to tell these delightful fables and to teach age-old lessons.

The Tortoise and the Hare

Materials: flannelboard, tortoise and hare cutouts (pattern page 51), fabric tree, long thin strip of fabric

Directions: Add fabric-paint faces on the tortoise and hare. Use the long thin strip for the race's finish line. Invite the children to supply the cheers of the crowd and to chant the closing line together.

One day Hare was bragging to all the animals. "I'm the fastest animal alive!" Just then Tortoise came by at his own steady pace. "Tortoise, you're the slowest animal! Don't you wish you were me–the fastest?"

"I may be slow, but I'm steady too. I just keep going and going," said Tortoise.

"Ha! Ha!" laughed Hare. "How about a race? The fastest and the steadiest. I bet I win. How about it?"

Tortoise agreed to race Hare. The other animals set the starting line, marked the course, and set up the finish line.

All the other animals shouted, "On your mark. Get set.

GO!" Hare took off at top speed. Tortoise plodded along at his own steady pace. When Hare looked behind him, he saw Tortoise getting smaller and smaller in the distance. Soon Hare couldn't see Tortoise anymore, so he stopped and rested against a tree. "Silly, Tortoise," Hare said. "Did he *really* think he could win this race?" Hare yawned and decided to take a little nap.

Tortoise plodded along at his own steady pace. He couldn't see Hare. "I'll just keep doing my best," he thought aloud.

When Hare woke up, he heard loud cheers. "What's that?" he wondered. When he looked down the road, there was Tortoise crossing over the finish line!

The crowd shouted, "Hooray for Tortoise! Slow but steady wins the race!"

The Dog and His Bone

Materials: flannelboard, dog cutout (pattern page 52), blue fabric strip, bone-shaped fabric

Directions: Add a fabric-paint face on the dog. Use the blue fabric for the river.

One day Dog, who was greedy and foolish, trotted along with a big bone in his mouth. He stopped at a river. When he looked in the water, he saw  another dog that looked like him. This other dog was holding a big bone. Dog growled, "Why should you have a bone that is bigger than mine?" But the other dog didn't answer. This made Dog angry. "Give me your bone!" barked Dog. When he opened his mouth wide to show his teeth, his bone dropped into the river! There had been no other dog. Just his own reflection!

The Ant and the Grasshopper

Directions: Add fabric-paint faces on the ant and grasshopper.

One day Grasshopper sat in the sun singing. She loved summer. "La, la, la!" she sang. Ant loved summer too. But she knew she had to work hard to collect food for winter.

Grasshopper saw Ant working. "Silly, Ant, come sing with me. Don't be so busy!"

"If all you do is sing now, you won't be prepared for winter," warned Ant.

"Silly, Ant, there's plenty of food around here now," replied Grasshopper. "La, la, la!" Grasshopper sang all summer and fall. Before she knew it, winter came and she had no food. Grasshopper tried to sing but was too weak. She dropped to the ground hungry and cold. "If only I had listened to Ant," she whispered. Just then Grasshopper saw Ant pass by with corn in her mouth. "Please, Ant, help me," called Grasshopper. "I promise that next summer I'll work hard to collect food for us both for the long winter." Ant took pity on Grasshopper and she shared her food.

That next summer Grasshopper was true to her word. She worked even harder than Ant preparing for winter!

The Ant and the Dove

Directions: Add fabric-paint faces on the ant, dove, and child. Add fabric clothes on the child.

One day Ant was very thirsty from working hard all day. He went to the river for a drink of water. Ant had just finished drinking when a small wave came up and carried him off. "Help! Help!" called Ant.

Dove, sitting in a tree, heard Ant's cries for help. She plucked a leaf from the tree and dropped it toward the river. The leaf floated to Ant. He climbed on it and paddled himself to shore. Ant was so tired that he rested awhile on the riverbank.

Ant was almost asleep when he heard footsteps. He saw a bird catcher ready to toss a net on Dove, who was sleeping in the tree. Ant raced to the bird catcher and bit his ankle. The bird catcher cried out in pain. Dove heard the cries and flew away to safety. Ant smiled. He was glad to help Dove, who had helped him!

The Shepherd and the Wolf

Materials: flannelboard, sheep cutout and wolf cutout (pattern page 53), child cutout (pattern page 50), fabric rectangles and triangles to create houses, pipe cleaner

Directions: Add fabric-paint faces on the sheep, wolf, and child. Add fabric clothes on the child. Form the pipe cleaner into a shepherd's crook, and attach it to the child's hand. Glue tufts of cotton to the sheep.

One day a shepherd boy was watching sheep on the hillside. "I'm bored. I need excitement," he said. So he thought of a plan. He ran into town and shouted, "Wolf! Wolf!"

The townspeople came running to help. When they reached the hillside, they asked, "Where's the wolf?"

The shepherd boy just laughed. "I was fooling you. There's no wolf!" The people were angry that the boy lied.

"You'll be sorry," they warned the boy. Then they all went back to town.

The next day the shepherd boy got bored again so he ran into town shouting, "Wolf! Wolf!"

The townspeople came running to help. When they reached the hillside, they asked, "Where's the wolf?"

The boy just laughed. "I was fooling you again. There's no wolf!" The people were very angry that the boy lied again.

"You'll be sorry," they warned the boy. Then they all went back to town.

The next day the shepherd boy was just getting bored when a real wolf came upon the sheep. He ran into town shouting, "Wolf! Wolf!" But the people didn't come running. They thought the boy was lying again. When the boy returned to his sheep, they had all been eaten.

The Fox and the Grapes

Materials: flannelboard, fox cutout and grapes cutout (pattern page 54), fabric tree

Directions: Add a fabric-paint face on the fox.

One hot day Fox sat down to rest under a tree. When he looked up, he saw a bunch of grapes hanging from a vine in the tree. "I'm so thirsty. I bet those grapes are juicy."

Fox stood up and tried to pick the grapes, but he couldn't reach them. He stood on the tips of his toes, but still he couldn't reach the grapes. He jumped as high as he could, but still he couldn't reach the grapes. He found a huge rock and slowly pushed it under the grapes. He stood on the rock on the tips of his toes, but still he couldn't reach the grapes. Poor Fox fell over! He dusted himself off and went on his way. "Who needs those grapes?" Fox muttered in anger. "I bet they're sour anyway!"

Fall Storytelling

Autumn is a time of crisp apples, crackling leaves, carved pumpkins, and more!

Four Red Apples

Materials: flannelboard, apple cutouts (pattern page 54), goat and hare cutouts (pattern page 51), pig cutout (pattern page 53), bear cutout (pattern page 52), fabric tree, fabric hill

Directions: Make a fabric tree. Cut out a cloud shape from green fabric and cut out a rectangle from brown fabric. Add a cotton beard on the goat. Use fabric paint to make faces and other details on the animals.

One fall day Bear stopped to rest under an apple tree that grew on a hill. Bear looked at the apples and licked his lips. "Mmm, the apples are ready to fall. When they do, they'll roll down the hill. How will I run after them? I'm too slow."

Just then Goat came by. "What are you doing under the apple tree?"

"I'm thinking of how to run after the apples when they fall and roll down the hill," replied Bear. "Can you run fast, Goat? Fast enough to catch the apples?"

Goat looked at the apples and licked his lips. "Watch me!" said Goat. Goat ran down and up the hill as fast as he could.

"Not fast enough, I'm afraid," said Bear. So Goat sat with Bear to help think.

Just then Pig came by. "What are you doing under the apple tree?"

"We're thinking of how to run after the apples when they fall and roll down the hill," replied Bear. "Can you run fast, Pig? Fast enough to catch the apples?

Pig looked at the apples and licked her lips. "Watch me!" said Pig. Pig ran down and up the hill as fast as she could.

"Not fast enough, I'm afraid," said Bear. So Pig sat down with Bear and Goat.

Just then Hare came by. "What are you doing under the apple tree?"

"We're thinking of how to run after the apples when they fall and roll down the hill," replied Bear. "Can you run fast, Hare? Fast enough to catch the apples?"

Hare looked at the apples and licked his lips. "Watch me!" said Hare. Hare ran down and up the hill as fast as he could.

The other animals cheered! "Hooray!" they shouted. "Hare can catch the apples!"

But when Hare ran to the animals, he tripped! "Ouch!" sobbed Hare. "My foot!"

"Oh, dear," said Bear sadly.

Holding his foot, Hare looked at the tree, looked at the animals, and looked down the hill. "Follow me," he said. So Bear, Goat, and Pig followed Hare to the bottom of the hill. "Let's wait," said Hare.

"For what?" asked Bear.

"You'll see," replied Hare. Soon after, all the apples fell from the tree and rolled quickly down the hill. Bear, Goat, Pig, and Hare were waiting. They caught them all!

Apple Seeds

Materials: flannelboard, large apple cutout (enlarge apple on pattern page 54), five fabric seeds, fabric tree

Directions: Repeat this story rhyme and let different children "plant" the seeds and make the tree grow.

Here's a big apple, red and round,
It grew from a tree out of the ground.

Inside the apple, crisp and sweet,
Are five tiny seeds, all nice and neat.

I'll plant all the seeds, one by one,
And let them all grow out in the sun.

I'll water the seeds, day by day,
And pull any weeds out of the way.

I watch all the seeds, brown and small,
Will one grow into a tree so tall?

Look! Here's a new plant, short and green,
The best apple tree I've ever seen!

Ten Crunchy Little Leaves

Materials: flannelboard, 10 leaf cutouts in fall colors (pattern page 54), fabric tree

Directions: Repeat this story rhyme and let different children remove leaves from the tree. Say a different child's name in each blank of the rhyme.

10 crunchy little leaves with colors so fine,
_____ caught one that fell; now there are nine.
9 crunchy little leaves near the garden gate,
_____ caught one that fell; now there are eight.
8 crunchy little leaves flutter toward Heaven,
_____ caught one that fell; now there are seven.
7 crunchy little leaves the color of sticks,
_____ caught one that fell; now there are six.
6 crunchy little leaves like to float and dive,
_____ caught one that fell; now there are five.
5 crunchy little leaves like to dip and soar,
_____ caught one that fell; now there are four.
4 crunchy little leaves wave hello to me,
_____ caught one that fell; now there are three.
3 crunchy little leaves the color of my shoe,
_____ caught one that fell; now there are two.
2 crunchy little leaves having so much fun,
_____ caught one that fell; now there is one.
1 crunchy little leaf flutters by itself,
_____ caught that leaf and put it on a shelf!

J330004 Creative Storytelling With Flannelboards

See the Pumpkin?

Materials: flannelboard, pumpkin cutout (enlarge pumpkin on pattern page 54), green strands of yarn, three leaf cutouts (pattern page 54), fabric seeds, small black fabric triangles and circles, black fabric mouth shapes

Directions: Repeat this story rhyme and let different children create the jack-o'-lantern's face. In the blank have the children use words such as the following to describe the face: funny, silly, scary, sad, happy.

See the pumpkin seeds?
See the pumpkin vine?
See the pumpkin growing?
I wish it were mine!

Buy the little pumpkin.
Take it home with me.
Carve a jack-o'-lantern,
As _____ as can be!

Five Little Pumpkins

Materials: flannelboard, five pumpkin cutouts (pattern page 54), fabric rectangle for the gate

Directions: Repeat this story rhyme and let different children roll the pumpkins off the gate.

Five little pumpkins sitting on a gate,
    The first one said, "Oh my, it's
        getting late!"
    The second one said, "Oh, look!
    I see a bat!"
    The third one said, "And there's a
silly hat!"
The fourth one said, "Let's run and run and run!"
The fifth one said, "I think Halloween is fun!"
"Woooooo" went the wind and out went the light,
And the five little pumpkins rolled out of sight!

Jack-O'

Materials: flannelboard, six pumpkin cutouts (pattern page 54), small black fabric triangles and circles, black fabric strips for mouths of jack-o'-lanterns, orange fabric pieces for cut-up pie, pie-shaped orange fabric

Directions: Repeat this story rhyme and let different children create each jack-o'-lantern's face described in the story.

Here is Jack-O'-Happy,
Here is Jack-O'-Sad,
Here is Jack-O'-Sleepy,
Here is Jack-O'-Mad,
Here is Jack-O'-Silly,
Here is Jack-O'-Shy,
Here are pumpkin pieces,
Here is pumpkin pie! Yum!

Little Turkey Lurkey

Materials: flannelboard, turkey cutout (pattern page 55), feather cutouts in various colors (pattern page 55)

Directions: Add fabric-paint details on the turkey. Teach the children the refrain. Let different children place feathers on the turkey's body.

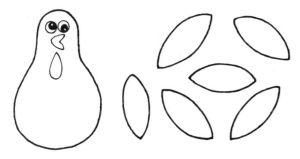

Little Turkey Lurkey strutting by a tree,
Looking for his feathers,
Calls out loud to me:

"Red, orange, and yellow,
Brown feathers too,
Thanksgiving time is almost here,
Oh, what am I to do?"

Little Turkey Lurkey searching far and near,
Looking for his feathers,
Whispers in my ear:

"Red, orange, and yellow,
Brown feathers too,
Thanksgiving time is almost here,
Oh, what am I to do?"

Little Turkey Lurkey running to and fro,
Looking for his feathers,
Finds them in a row!

"Red, orange, and yellow,
Brown feathers too,
Thanksgiving time is almost here,
I'm ready now. Are you?"

Five Pilgrim Children

Materials: flannelboard; five child cutouts (pattern page 50); cornbread, cooked turkey, nuts, popcorn, and pie cutouts (pattern page 55)

Directions: Use fabric paint to make faces and other details on the child cutouts. Add fabric clothing so that the cutouts look like Pilgrims. Use fabric paint to add details to the food. Repeat this story rhyme and let different children match a food cutout with each child cutout.

Five Pilgrim children on Thanksgiving Day,
The first one said, "I'll have cornbread if I may."
The second one said, "I'll have turkey hot and roasted."
The third one said, "I'll have nuts warm and toasted."
The fourth one said, "I'll have popcorn puffed up high."
The fifth one said, "I'll have yummy pumpkin pie!"

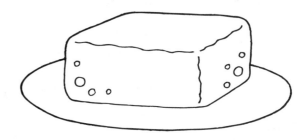

Winter Storytelling

Holiday lights and frosty delights are all part of this season.

Build a Snowman

Materials: flannelboard; three large, white fabric circles in varying sizes; top hat cutout (pattern page 56); narrow orange fabric; 10 tiny circles of black fabric for stones; red fabric strip; sun cutout (pattern page 56)

Six Silly Snowmen

Materials: flannelboard; six snowman cutouts, one sun cutout, and six top hat cutouts (pattern page 56)

Directions: Add fabric-paint details on the snowmen. Add top hats. Let the children take turns removing the snowmen as they "melt."

Six silly snowmen standing in the sun,
Saying, "Yippee! Yippee! Yee!
We're having so much fun!"
The sun came out to brighten the day,
And one little snowman melted away.

Five silly snowmen standing in the sun, (*and so on*)

One silly snowman standing in the sun,
Saying, "Yippee! Yippee! Yee!
I'm having so much fun!"
The sun came out to brighten the day,
And the one little snowman melted away.

Directions: Repeat this story rhyme and let different children build the snowman.

Take three snowballs, big and round,
And build a snowman on the ground,
Put a top hat on his head,
Give him a scarf all bright and red.

Take a carrot for his face,
And make a nose in the right place,
Put two stones for his two eyes,
Give him a smile, all kind and wise.

Take some round stones, one-two-three,
And make three buttons you can see,
Put your snowman in the sun,
Give him a pat, your work is done!

Wintertime

Directions: Add fabric-paint details on the animals. Let the children take turns placing a snowflake on the flannelboard each time the word snowflake is spoken. Let the children count the snowflakes.

Wintertime is snowflake time,
When bears take winter rests,
Wintertime is snowflake time,
When ants keep warm in nests.

Wintertime is snowflake time,
When robins fly away,
Wintertime is snowflake time,
When cold is here to stay!

"Let's Dress for Wintertime" Song

Materials: flannelboard, snow clothing cutouts (pattern page 57), child cutout (enlarge pattern page 50)

Directions: Sing the song to the tune of "The Farmer in the Dell." Add fabric-paint details on the clothing and the child. Let the children take turns placing the clothing in sequence on the child.

Let's dress for wintertime,
Let's dress for wintertime,
Heigh, ho, the snow is cold,
Let's dress for wintertime.

We'll put our snow pants on, . . .

We'll put our snow boots on, . . .

We'll put our jackets on, . . .

We'll put our snow hats on, . . .

We'll put our mittens on, . . .

Holiday Candles

Materials: flannelboard, eight candle cutouts and eight flame cutouts (pattern page 61)

Directions: Let the children take turns placing the candles in a row and counting the candles aloud. Let the children take turns "lighting" each candle by placing a flame cutout above a candle. Have some children say the wind's part and some children shout "Eeek!" Let other children take away the flames when the candles "flicker and go out."

Holiday candles lining up so straight—
One, two, three, four, five, six, seven, eight!
Holiday candles standing in a row,
Light all the candles and watch them glow!

"Oooooo" went the winter wind,
"Eeek!" I did shout,
    And the holiday candles,
        Flickered and went out!

Little Cookie

Materials: flannelboard, large brown fabric circle, child cutout (pattern page 50), tiny fabric shapes in a variety of colors

Directions: Use the circle for the plain cookie. Let the children take turns "decorating" the cookie with the tiny fabric shapes.

There was a little cookie as plain as could be,
All day it cried and sobbed, "Oh, pity, poor plain me."
A little child was listening to the cookie's cries,
And gathered up the gumdrops and other sweet supplies.
    The child sprinkled this and that until the day was done,
        The cookie smiled and shouted out, "Aren't I the fancy one?"

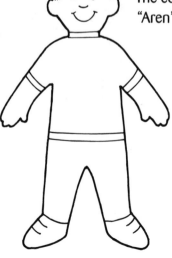

The Lost Hat

Materials: flannelboard; snowman, sun, and top hat cutouts (pattern page 56), wind cutout (pattern page 57)

Directions: Use fabric paint to add details to the cutouts. Let the children help you manipulate the cutouts.

One cold day Snowman was watching Winter Wind play tricks on the snowflakes. Winter Wind would blow and blow so hard that the snowflakes would fly up and flutter in the air. "Winter Wind, you are quite a trickster," said Snowman. "I'm glad you can't play tricks on me!"

"Oooo!" howled Winter Wind. Suddenly the wind blew harder. Snowman began to shake and shiver. "Stop that, Winter Wind!" Just then Snowman's hat blew off! "My hat! Where's my hat?"

But "Oooo" was all Winter Wind would say as he blew and blew. Then he blew away.

Soon Sun came out. "Sun, Winter Wind played a trick on me and blew my hat away. I asked him where he blew my hat, but all he said was 'Oooo!'"

Sun laughed. "Winter Wind is quite a trickster. Let's play a trick on him!"

After Sun hid way up in the sky, Snowman called to Winter Wind, "Winter Wind! Please come here and play tricks on the snowflakes again."

When Winter Wind came blowing in, Snowman said, "One last time, Winter Wind, where's my hat?" But "Oooo" was all Winter Wind would say as he blew and blew and blew.

"All right, Winter Wind," said Snowman. "I bet I can trick you so you can't blow and do your tricks. If I do, will you give me back my hat?"

"Oooo," howled Winter Wind.

So Snowman started moving his arms up and down while Sun silently hid behind Winter Wind. When Winter Wind started to blow, he couldn't! Sun had warmed up the air too much! Winter Wind tried and tried, but he couldn't blow.

"Oooo," howled Winter Wind. Then he swooped down to show Snowman where his hat was. It was hiding *behind* Snowman this whole time!

Snowman and Sun began to laugh! Winter Wind looked up. He saw Sun hiding behind him! Winter Wind began to laugh too. What tricks they had played on each other! Winter Wind had hid Snowman's hat behind Snowman. And Snowman had hid Sun behind Winter Wind!

Spring Storytelling

This time of year is filled with flower buds, baby animals, and pattering rain.

Three Tiny Seeds

Materials: flannelboard, three fabric flower seeds, 18 flower cutouts (three each of red, orange, white, blue, brown, and pink; pattern page 58)

Directions: Line up three fabric seeds on the flannelboard. Have the children recite this rhyme. Then have them cover their eyes. Choose one child to place one color of flower over each seed on the flannelboard. With their eyes still closed, let the other children guess which color flower "grew." Repeat this story rhyme and let different children "grow" the flowers.

Three tiny seeds all planted in a row,
Which color flowers do you think will grow?
Red, orange, or white,
Blue, brown, or pink?
Cover up your eyes now,
And help me think!

The Snowdrifts Are Melting

Materials: flannelboard, several pieces of white fabric shaped like snowdrifts, variety of cutouts (one for each snowdrift; pattern pages 50–64)

Directions: Add fabric-paint details to the cutouts. Hide a cutout under each snowdrift. As the children recite this rhyme, let different children lift up each snowdrift to discover what's hidden! Repeat this rhyme and choose children to hide the items under the snowdrifts.

The snowdrifts are melting,
Around you and me.
What's under this one?
A _____ we see!

The snowdrifts are melting,
Around you and me.
What's under this one?
A _____ we see!

(Repeat the verse as often as you want.)

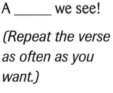

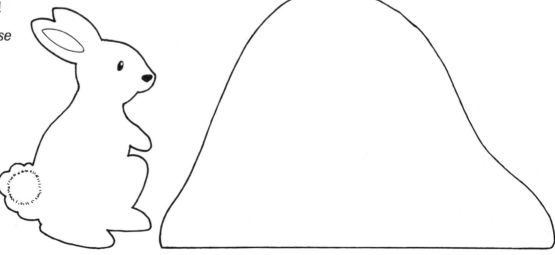

I Had a Little Puppy

Materials: flannelboard, dog cutout (pattern page 52), child cutout (pattern page 50), bee and bunny cutouts (pattern page 58), bird cutout (pattern page 53)

Directions: Add fabric-paint details on the child and animal cutouts. Attach fabric clothing on the child. Let the children take turns moving the puppy next to each animal and next to the child while the other children recite the rhyme.

> I had a little puppy whose coat was fluffy brown,
> He played all day and followed me all over town.
> He barked at a bunny,
> He barked at a bee,
> He barked at a bluebird,
> And he barked at me!
> He chased that old bunny,
> He chased that old bee,
> He chased that old bluebird,
> And he chased after me!

Flying Kites

Materials: flannelboard; four child cutouts (pattern page 50); four fabric kite shapes (use solid color fabrics); red, brown, black, and yellow yarn

Directions: Add fabric-paint details on each child cutout (make two boys and two girls). Add fabric-paint details and yarn tails on the kites. Attach fabric clothing on each child cutout. Place a different color of yarn hair on the head of each cutout to match the rhyme. As the children recite this rhyme, let them choose which color kite to name in the blank. Then let the children take turns matching the correct kite with each child.

> A girl with red hair jumped so high,
> She flew with her _____ kite up in the sky!
>
> A boy with brown hair jumped so high,
> He flew with his _____ kite up in the sky!
>
> A girl with black hair jumped so high,
> She flew with her _____ kite up in the sky!
>
> A boy with yellow hair jumped so high,
> He flew with his _____ kite up in the sky!

One Drop, Two Drops

Materials: flannelboard, raindrop and umbrella cutouts (pattern page 59)

Directions: Add fabric-paint details on the umbrella. Let the children take turns placing a certain number of raindrops on top of the umbrella. Have the rest of the children count the drops.

One drop, two drops, three drops, four,
Five drops, six drops, seven drops, more!
Eight drops, nine drops, ten drops, stop!
How many drops hit my umbrella top?

Five Tiny Ducklings

Materials: flannelboard, six duck cutouts (use black fabric and enlarge one for the mother; pattern page 59), sun cutout (pattern page 56)

Directions: Add fabric-paint details on the ducklings and mother duck. Let the children take turns moving the the ducklings next to the mother duck. After each verse, move the mother duck and sun cutouts and remove one duckling.

Five tiny ducklings with feathers so black,
Sang, "Wibble, wobble, wibble, wobble,
Quack, quack, quack!"
Mama called the ducklings to sit in the sun,
"Come, little ducklings! Run, run, run!"

Four tiny ducklings with feathers so black,
Sang, "Wibble, wobble, wibble, wobble,
Quack, quack, quack!"
Mama called the ducklings to sit in the sun,
"Come, little ducklings! Run, run, run!" (*and so on*)

One tiny duckling with feathers so black,
Sang, "Wibble, wobble, wibble, wobble,
Quack, quack, quack!"
Mama called the duckling to sit in the sun,
"Come, little duckling! Run, run, run!"

And they sat in the sun singing, "Quack! Quack! Quack!"

Out Hatched a ____ for Me!

Materials: flannelboard, three large fabric egg shapes in varying sizes, duck cutout (pattern page 59), bird cutout (pattern page 53), tortoise cutout (pattern page 51)

Directions: Add fabric-paint details on the eggs and animals. The first time hide one animal cutout under each egg. As the children recite the rhyme, lift up the egg to reveal what's hidden. Let the children take turns hiding the animals under the eggs.

> I found a big egg as pretty as could be,
> And when it cracked and opened up,
> Out hatched a _____ for me!
>
> I found a bigger egg as pretty as could be,
> And when it cracked and opened up,
> Out hatched a _____ for me!
>
> I found the biggest egg as pretty as could be,
> And when it cracked and opened up,
> Out hatched a _____ for me!

The Itsy Bitsy Spider

Materials: flannelboard, spider and raindrop cutouts (pattern page 59), sun cutout (pattern page 56), long fabric rectangle

Directions: Add fabric-paint details on the spider. Use the rectangle for the waterspout. Let the children take turns manipulating the spider as the rest of the children recite this old-time favorite rhyme.

> The itsy bitsy spider,
> Climbed up the waterspout,
> Down came the rain,
> And washed the spider out!
> Out came the sun,
> And dried up all the rain,
> And the itsy bitsy spider,
> Climbed up the spout again!

Summer Storytelling

Puffy clouds, buzzing bees, sandy beaches, and more fill up summer days.

White Cloud, White Cloud

Materials: flannelboard, several cutouts made from white fabric (pattern pages 50–64)

Directions: Let the children take turns pointing to a cloud shape on the flannelboard each time the verse is recited. Afterward, take the children outdoors to name cloud shapes in the sky! You might have the children recite the verse outside and have volunteers name cloud shapes they see.

White cloud, white cloud,
Moving through the sky.
What do you look like,
Floating way up high?

_____ (children's answer)

Buzzing Bees

Materials: flannelboard; 1 beehive cutout and 10 to 20 bee cutouts (pattern page 58)

Directions: Use fabric paint to add details to the beehive and the bees. Hide some bees under the beehive. Have the children recite this rhyme. Choose a child to lift the beehive and have the children count the bees hiding. Repeat this rhyme and let the children take turns hiding the bees each time you say the verse.

Here is the beehive, but where are the bees?
Hidden away where nobody sees.
Lift up the beehive. Count all the bees.
Buzz! Buzz! Buzz! How many please?

(Children count the number of bees hidden under the hive.)

Ten Funny Fishes

Materials: flannelboard, 10 fish cutouts (pattern page 60)

Directions: Use fabric paint to add details to the fish. Line up the 10 fish on the flannelboard. Let the children take turns removing a fish with each verse.

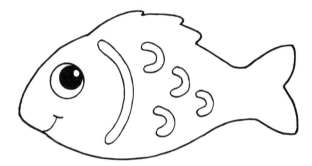

Ten funny fishes swimming in a brook,
One swam next to me and bit my little hook!
Away swam the fishes with a splish, splish, splash!
Away from my boat the fishes made a dash!

Nine funny fishes swimming in a brook,
One swam next to me and bit my little hook!
Away swam the fishes with a splish, splish, splash!
Away from my boat the fishes made a dash!

Eight funny fishes swimming in a brook, *(and so on)*

One funny fish swimming in a brook,
It swam next to me and *saw* my little hook!
Away swam the fish with a splish, splish, splash!
Away from my boat the fish made a dash!

When We Go to the Beach

Materials: flannelboard; shovel, pail, swimsuit, sunglasses, sandals, sun hat, and beachball cutouts (pattern page 60); fabric rectangle towel; piece of fabric shaped like a sack

Directions: Use fabric paint to add details to the cutouts. Let the children take turns "packing for the beach" by placing three cutouts on the sack while the rest of the children recite the rhyme.

When we go to the beach,
We'll take a sack,
When we go to the beach,
Here's what we'll pack—
A _____ and a _____ and a _____.
That's three!
These are the things we'll take to the sea!

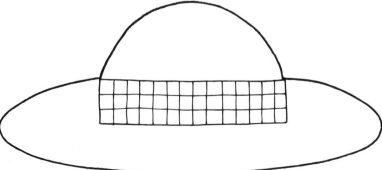

Ten on the Sand

Materials: flannelboard, 10 seashell cutouts (pattern page 64), long strip of light brown fabric, long strip of blue fabric

Directions: Use fabric paint to add details to the seashells. Place the brown fabric strip on the flannelboard to represent the sand at the beach. Line up the 10 seashells on the "sand." Place the blue strip near the sand. The blue represents the ocean. Let the children take turns moving a seashell under the sea with each verse.

There were ten on the sand,
And I heard one command,
"Move over! Move over!"
So they all moved over,
And one washed away,

There were nine on the sand,
And I heard one command, (*and so on*)

There was one on the sand,
And I heard it command,
"Yippee! The beach is all mine!"

Hot Days, Lazy Days

Materials: flannelboard, winter clothes cutouts (pattern page 57), summer clothes cutouts (pattern page 60)

Directions: Use fabric paint to add details to the winter and summer clothing. Mix up all the cutouts on the flannelboard. Recite the verse. Let the children take turns sorting the clothing into winter and summer attire. Have the children name the clothing.

Hot days, lazy days,
Summer is such fun!
Oh, what should we wear,
To play in the sun?

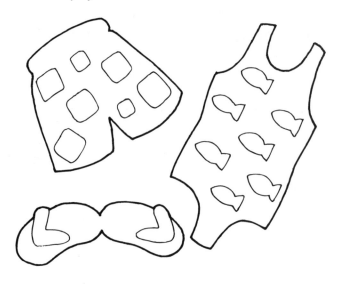

A Little Girl/Boy Went Walking

Materials: flannelboard, several of the smaller beach-related cutouts (pattern page 60), several seashell cutouts (pattern page 64), two child cutouts (enlarge pattern page 50), large pocket-shaped piece of fabric

Directions: Use fabric paint to add details to the cutouts. Make one child a girl and one child a boy. Attach fabric summer clothing to the children. Place all the beach and seashell cutouts on the flannelboard with either the boy or girl cutout. As you tell the story, let the children take turns hiding beach items under the large pocket. After each telling, let the children count and name the items hidden!

A little girl/boy went walking out upon the sand,
The little girl/boy saw many things,
And held them in her/his hand.
She/He put some in her/his pocket,
And tucked them safe inside,
Oh, do you know what she/he saw,
And all that she/he did hide?

We're Going on a Picnic

Materials: flannelboard, several food cutouts (pattern pages 54–55, 63), large fabric rectangle

Directions: Use fabric paint to add details to the food cutouts. The rectangle will be the picnic blanket on which the children place the food items in sequence as the verses are recited. Place all the food cutouts on the flannelboard, or give each child a food cutout to place on the flannelboard as this rhyme is recited. (Say a different child's name for each blank in a verse.)

REFRAIN

We're going on a picnic,
    We'll bring good things to eat.
    We're going on a picnic,
    Who will bring a treat?

_____ will bring the apples,
Ooh! What a treat!
_____ will bring the apples,
All for us to eat!

REPEAT THE REFRAIN

_____ will bring bananas,
Ooh! What a treat!
_____ will bring bananas,
All for us to eat!

REPEAT THE REFRAIN

(Make up verses with each child's name and a food to bring on the picnic!)

All-About-Me Storytelling

Directions: When a child has a birthday, have the rest of the children recite this story to the birthday child before singing "Happy Birthday!" Let the birthday child place on the flannelboard all the birthday cutouts in sequence as the story is told. (Have ready fabric "sprinkles" and other fabric cake decorations. Let the birthday child decorate the fabric cake!)

Hip! Hip! Hooray!

Materials: flannelboard; cutouts for flour bag, sugar bag, egg, salt container, milk carton, mixing bowl, cake pan, frosting container, cake, and candle (pattern page 61); tiny fabric shapes to use as "cake decorations"

_____ has a birthday,
A birthday, a birthday,
_____ has a birthday,
Hip! Hip! Hooray!

Let's bake a big cake,
A big cake, a big cake,
Let's bake a big cake,
Hip! Hip! Hooray!

Let's pour the flour,
The flour, the flour,
Let's pour the flour,
Hip! Hip! Hooray!

Let's crack a big egg,
A big egg, a big egg,
Let's crack a big egg,
Hip! Hip! Hooray!

Let's sprinkle sugar,
Sugar, sugar,
Let's sprinkle sugar,
Hip! Hip! Hooray!

Let's shake some sea salt,
Sea salt, sea salt,
Let's shake some sea salt,
Hip! Hip! Hooray!

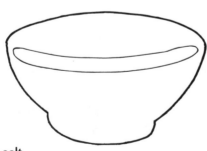

Let's pour some fresh milk,
Fresh milk, fresh milk,
Let's pour some fresh milk,
Hip! Hip! Hooray!

Let's mix the batter,
Batter, batter,
Let's mix the batter,
Hip! Hip! Hooray!

Let's let the cake bake,
Cake bake, cake bake,
Let's let the cake bake,
Hip! Hip! Hooray!

Let's let the cake cool,
Cake cool, cake cool,
Let's let the cake cool,
Hip! Hip! Hooray!

Let's frost the cool cake,
Cool cake, cool cake,
Let's frost the cool cake,
Hip! Hip! Hooray!

Let's put on the candles,
Candles, candles,
Let's put on the candles,
Hip! Hip! Hooray!

Let's sing to _____,
To _____, to _____,
Let's sing to _____,
Hip! Hip! Hooray!

I Have a Little Feeling

Materials: flannelboard, heart cutout (pattern page 58), mini-sentence strips, Velcro ("hooks" strip)

Directions: Write the name of a feeling—*sad, happy, shy, embarrassed, angry, excited, loved*—on separate sentence strips. Attach a "hooks" piece of self-sticking Velcro to the back of each strip. Place one strip underneath the heart on the flannelboard. Have the children tell this story with you. At the end of the story, lift up the heart and read the emotion. Have the children show the emotion in their faces. Repeat the story and let the children take turns placing a sentence strip under the heart.

I have a little feeling,
That rolls around in me,
It likes to hide inside my heart,
So no one else will see,

But when this little feeling,
Decides to come outside,
It tumbles out across my face,
And doesn't try to hide!

I'm feeling ____.

Mister Alligator

Materials: flannelboard, alligator cutout (pattern page 50), variety of animal cutouts (pattern pages 50–64)

Directions: Use fabric paint to add details to the animals. Place the alligator on the flannelboard. Have the children tell this story with you. Let the children fill in each blank with a different animal's name. Let the children take turns placing each animal in sequence next to the alligator.

Mister alligator,
Wished he had a friend.
He searched high and low,
He searched end to end.

Soon came a(n)_____,
Walking round the bend,
"Hello!" said Alligator,
"Will you be my friend?"

Soon came a(n)_____,
Walking round the bend,
"Hello!" said Alligator,
"Will you be my friend?" (*keep repeating verse*)

Mister Alligator,
Played and played all day,
"Friends," said Alligator,
"Are the best in every way!"

Body Language

Use the rhyme and song below to reinforce children's knowledge of body part names.

Materials: flannelboard, child cutouts (enough so each child has one; pattern page 50)

Directions: Use fabric paint to add details to the child cutouts. Give each child a child cutout. Teach the children the story or song. Let each child have a turn placing his or her cutout on the flannelboard and pointing to each area or body part on the cutout as it is said aloud in the story or song.

I Have a Healthy Body

I have a healthy body,
With heart and lungs and hips,
Stomach, ribs, kneecaps, brain,
Neck and chin and lips.

I have a healthy body,
With eyes and ears and nose,
Fingers, hands, shoulders, arms,
Legs and feet and toes.

"Head, Shoulders, Knees, and Toes" Song

Head, shoulders, knees, and toes,
Knees and toes,
Head, shoulders, knees, and toes,
Knees and toes,
Eyes and ears and mouth and nose,
Head, shoulders, knees, and toes,
Knees and toes!

"I Am Special" Song

Materials: flannelboard, variety of cutouts (pattern pages 50–64)

Directions: Use fabric paint to add details to the cutouts. Place all the cutouts on the flannelboard. Invite one child at a time up to the board and have the children sing this song (sung to the tune of "Are You Sleeping?") to him or her. Tell the celebrated child to pick out which items on the flannelboard he or she likes best. Have the child hold up one or two and explain his or her decision.

> You are special! You are special!
> Yes, you are! Yes, you are!
> Show us what you like, please,
> Show us now and don't tease,
> _____ _____, _____ _____! *(Repeat child's full name.)*

Manners

Materials: flannelboard, four child cutouts (pattern page 50), mini-sentence strips, self-sticking Velcro

Directions: Use fabric paint to add details to the cutouts. Print the words *Thank you*, *Please*, and *Bless you* on separate sentence strips. Attach a piece of self-sticking Velcro to the back of each strip. Line up the child cutouts on the flannelboard. Randomly place the sentence strips. As you tell this story, place the matching sentence strip with each child in order. Let the children take turns matching the words with the child cutouts as you retell this simple tale.

> This little child said, "Thank you."
> This little child said, "Please."
> This little child said, "Bless you,"
> When this little child did sneeze!
> *A-a-a-a-a-ah choooo!*

Storytelling About Animals

Children will enjoy rhymes and tales about wild animals, farm critters, and pets.

Hey, Diddle Diddle

Materials: flannelboard; moon, fiddle, dish, spoon, and cat cutouts (pattern page 62); dog cutout (pattern page 52)

Directions: Use fabric paint to add details to the cutouts. Let the children take turns manipulating the cutouts while the rest of the children say this rhyme.

Hey, diddle, diddle,
The cat and the fiddle,
The cow jumped over the moon,
The little dog laughed
To see such sport,
And the dish ran away with the spoon!

One Bear, Two Bears . . .

Materials: flannelboard, 10 bear cutouts (pattern page 52), large fabric rectangle

Directions: Use fabric paint to add details to the bears. Hide the bears under the fabric rectangle "door." Let the children take turns opening the door and lining up the bears while the rest of the children tell this tale.

One bear, two bears, three bears, four,
Five bears, six bears,
Coming out the door!
Seven bears, eight bears, nine bears, ten,
Let's count the bears,
Together again!

Dog, the Bravest Animal

Materials: flannelboard, dog and bear cutouts (pattern page 52), hare cutout (pattern page 51), fox cutout (pattern page 54), cat cutout (pattern page 62), three pink fabric circles in varying sizes

Directions: Use fabric paint to add details to the cutouts. Use the circles for the ever-enlarging bubble gum.

Once upon a time, Dog thought he was the bravest animal. Dog wouldn't help or play with anyone. He just bragged. Soon the town animals hid whenever Dog came near. So Dog set off for the country. On the path he sniffed something sweet and sticky. Without thinking, Dog popped it in his mouth. "Mmm," said Dog. "I *must* be brave to do something without thinking." And he started to chew the sweet lump.

Soon Hare came along. "Hello! Who are you?" asked Hare.

Dog tried to open his mouth but his teeth were stuck! "Mmffzzz!" said Dog.

"Well, Mmffzzz, I'm glad you're not Dog!" said Hare. "I hear he brags too much. Say, may I play with you?"

"Mmffzzz," was all Dog could say as he ran off with Hare.

Soon Bear came along. "Hello!" said Bear. "Who are you?" he said to Dog.

Dog tried again to open his mouth, but "Mmffzzz," was all Dog could say.

"Well, Mmffzzz, I'm glad you're not Dog!" said Bear. "I hear he brags too much. Say, may I play with you?"

"Mmffzzz," was all Dog could say as he ran off with Hare and Bear.

Soon Fox came along. "Hello!" said Fox. "Who are you?" he said to Dog.

Dog tried harder to open his mouth but "Mmffzzz," was all Dog could say.

"Well, Mmffzzz, I'm glad you're not Dog!" said Fox. "I hear he brags too much. Say, may I play with you?"

"Mmffzzz," was all Dog could say as he ran off with Hare and Bear and Fox.

Hare, Bear, Fox, and Dog were having fun when they heard a cry. They followed the sound and found Cat trapped under a branch. "Help me!" cried Cat. Without thinking, Dog lifted up the branch and carried Cat to safety.

"Hooray for Mmffzzz!" shouted the animals. "You are the bravest of all!"

"Mmffzzz?" Cat said. "I don't know any Mmffzzz. But I do want to thank Dog for saving my life. I thought I'd never say this, but will you be my friend, Dog?

"Dog!" shouted the animals. "*This* is Dog?" they all said together. Then they stared at Dog, who was struggling so hard to open his mouth. He started huffing and puffing! He huffed so hard that a bubble started coming out of his mouth. Soon the bubble got so big it burst! POP! There was pink gooey stuff all over his face!

Dog sighed, "I may not be the bravest animal there is but I *am* the silliest." Then he started to laugh. The other animals laughed with him!

Chicken Little

Materials: flannelboard, chick and hen cutouts (pattern page 63), rooster cutout (pattern page 59), turkey cutout (pattern page 55), duck cutout (pattern page 59), owl cutout (pattern page 51), apple cutout (pattern page 54), fabric tree

Directions: Use fabric paint to add details to the cutouts. Let the children help you manipulate the cutouts as you tell this favorite animal tale.

Once upon a time, Chicken Little was scratching for food near an apple tree. Suddenly, Chicken Little heard a crack! An apple fell on her head. Plop! Then the apple rolled in the grass. "Ouch!" cried Chicken Little. "Oh, dear! The sky is falling! I must go tell the king."

Away ran Chicken Little as fast as she could. Soon she met Henny Penny. "Why are you running so fast?" asked Henny Penny.

"The sky is falling! I must go tell the king," said Chicken Little.

"How do you know the sky is falling?" asked Henny Penny.

"I heard the sky crack. I felt a piece of it hit my head," said Chicken Little.

"Then I will go with you to tell the king!" said Henny Penny.

Away ran Chicken Little and Henny Penny as fast as they could. Soon they met Cocky Locky. "Why are you running so fast?" asked Cocky Locky.

"The sky is falling! I must go tell the king," said Chicken Little.

"How do you know the sky is falling?" asked Cocky Locky.

"I heard the sky crack. I felt a piece of it hit my head," said Chicken Little.

"Then I will go with you to tell the king!" said Cocky Locky.

Away ran Chicken Little, Henny Penny, and Cocky Locky as fast as they could. Soon they met Turkey Lurkey. "Why are you running so fast?" asked Turkey Lurkey.

"The sky is falling! I must go tell the king," said Chicken Little.

"How do you know the sky is falling?" asked Turkey Lurkey.

"I heard the sky crack. I felt a piece of it hit my head," said Chicken Little.

"Then I will go with you to tell the king!" said Turkey Lurkey.

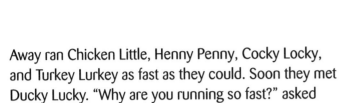

Away ran Chicken Little, Henny Penny, Cocky Locky, and Turkey Lurkey as fast as they could. Soon they met Ducky Lucky. "Why are you running so fast?" asked Ducky Lucky.

"The sky is falling! I must go tell the king," said Chicken Little.

"How do you know the sky is falling?" asked Ducky Lucky.

"I heard the sky crack. I felt a piece of it hit my head," said Chicken Little.

"Then I will go with you to tell the king!" said Ducky Lucky.

Away ran Chicken Little, Henny Penny, Cocky Locky, Turkey Lurkey, and Ducky Lucky as fast as they could. Soon they met Wise Owl. "Why are you running so fast?" asked Wise Owl.

"The sky is falling! I must go tell the king," said Chicken Little.

"How do you know the sky is falling?" asked Wise Owl.

"I heard the sky crack. I felt a piece of it hit my head," said Chicken Little.

"Then show me where the sky fell before you tell the king," said Wise Owl.

So Chicken Little led the way. Henny Penny, Cocky Locky, Turkey Lurkey, Ducky Lucky, and Wise Owl followed her. Soon they came to the apple tree. "The sky cracked right here," said Chicken Little. "Then a piece of it fell down and hit my head. It rolled in the grass somewhere."

Chicken Little was still a bit shaken by what had happened to her so she rested under the tree while the other animals searched for the piece of sky.

"Here it is!" cried Wise Owl. Henny Penny, Cocky Locky, Turkey Lurkey, and Ducky Lucky stared at the apple. Then they all looked at Chicken Little. One by one the animals walked away. Wise Owl stayed behind.

"Chicken Little, the sky didn't fall," said Wise Owl. "An apple fell and hit your head. If you are a smart little chicken, you will come here and eat this delicious apple before the other animals decide how good it would taste for lunch."

And that is what Chicken Little did. She pecked and pecked and pecked at the apple until just the seeds lay on the ground. "I'm glad it wasn't the sky," said Chicken Little. "Apples taste much better!"

J330004 Creative Storytelling With Flannelboards

Fuzzy Caterpillars

Materials: flannelboard, two caterpillar cutouts and two chrysalis cutouts (pattern page 64), leaf cutout (pattern page 54), two tiny white fabric eggs, four heart cutouts (pattern page 58), two long oval pieces of fabric

Directions: Use fabric paint to add details to the cutouts. Make each butterfly by gluing the points of two heart cutouts together and attaching on top a long oval for the body. Let the children take turns manipulating the cutouts while you tell this tale.

Fuzzy caterpillars,
Hatching from white eggs,
Out upon a leaf,
Crept with tiny legs.

Fuzzy caterpillars,
Growing very fat,
Out upon a leaf,
Ate all this and that.

Fuzzy caterpillars,
Hanging upside down,
Out upon a leaf,
Formed a skin so brown.

Fuzzy caterpillars,
Hiding in disguise,
Out upon a leaf,
Changed to butterflies!

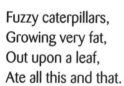

Mama Frog

Materials: flannelboard, three tadpole cutouts and three frog cutouts (pattern page 64), three tiny white fabric eggs

Directions: Use fabric paint to add details to the cutouts. Let the children take turns manipulating the cutouts while you tell this tale.

"Mama Frog, Mama Frog,
Where are your tiny eggs?"
  "Hatching, hatching!"
Shh! Shh! Shh!

"Mama Frog, Mama Frog,
Where are your tadpoles?"
  "Swimming, swimming!"
Splash, splash, splash!

"Mama Frog, Mama Frog,
Where are your little frogs?"
  "Eating, eating!"
Croak! Croak! Croak!

Old Farmer Brown

Materials: flannelboard, duck cutouts (pattern page 59), chick cutouts (pattern page 63), horse cutouts (pattern page 56), goose cutouts (pattern page 64), cow cutouts (pattern page 50), pig cutouts (pattern page 53), child cutouts (use one child cutout for Old Farmer Brown; pattern page 50)

Directions: Make several of each cutout. Use fabric paint to add details to the cutouts. Let the children take turns manipulating the cutouts while you tell this tale.

Old Farmer Brown called out one day,
"White ducks, white ducks, come my way!"
With a quack quack here,
And a waddle waddle there,
Soon there were white ducks everywhere!

Old Farmer Brown called out one day,
"Chickens, chickens, come my way!"
With a cluck cluck here,
And a peck peck there,
Soon there were chickens everywhere!

Old Farmer Brown called out one day,
"Horses, horses, come my way!"
With a neigh neigh here,
And a trot trot there,
Soon there were horses everywhere!

Old Farmer Brown called out one day,
"White geese, white geese, come my way!"
With a honk honk here,
And a wobble wobble there,
Soon there were white geese everywhere!

Old Farmer Brown called out one day,
"Milk cows, milk cows, come my way!"
With a moo moo here,
And a sway sway there,
Soon there were milk cows everywhere!

Old Farmer Brown called out one day,
"Pink pigs, pink pigs, come my way!"
With an oink oink here,
And a slop slop there,
Soon there were pink pigs everywhere!
(Make up some of your own verses.)

Old Farmer Brown called out one day,
"Children, children, come my way!"
With a giggle giggle here,
And a run run there,
Soon there were
children everywhere!

Little Red Hen

Materials: flannelboard; hen cutout (pattern page 63); goose cutout (pattern page 64); rooster cutout (pattern page 59); turkey cutout (pattern page 55); duck cutout (pattern page 59); flour, egg, milk, sugar, mixing bowl, cake pan, and cake cutouts (pattern page 61); fabric strips for the wheat; yellow fabric rectangle for butter

Directions: Use fabric paint to add details to the cutouts. Let the children help you manipulate the cutouts as you tell this favorite animal tale.

Once upon a time, a little red hen was scratching for food in a field when she found some grains of wheat. "Who will help me plant this wheat?" asked Little Red Hen.

"Not I," said the goose.

"Not I," said the duck.

"Not I," said the rooster.

"Not I," said the turkey.

"Then I will have to plant it myself," said the little red hen. So she planted the wheat in the garden.

"Who will help me water the wheat?" asked the little red hen.

"Not I," said the goose.

"Not I," said the duck.

"Not I," said the rooster.

"Not I," said the turkey.

"Then I will have to water it myself," said the little red hen. So she watered the wheat every morning. Soon the wheat grew tall and ripe.

"Who will help me cut the wheat?" asked the little red hen.

"Not I," said the goose.

"Not I," said the duck.

"Not I," said the rooster.

"Not I," said the turkey.

"Then I will have to cut it myself," said the little red hen. So she chopped and chopped until the wheat was all cut down.

"Who will help me take the wheat to the mill?" asked the little red hen.

"Not I," said the goose.

"Not I," said the duck.

"Not I," said the rooster.

"Not I," said the turkey.

"Then I will have to take it myself," said the little red hen. So she took the wheat to the mill to be ground into flour.

Later the little red hen came back to the farm with a big bag of fine white flour. "Who will help me make a cake from this fine white flour?" asked the little red hen.

"Not I," said the goose.

"Not I," said the duck.

"Not I," said the rooster.

"Not I," said the turkey.

"Then I will have to make it myself," said the little red hen. So she mixed the flour with eggs and milk and sugar and butter. She poured the cake batter into a pan and put it in a hot oven to bake.

Soon the whole farmyard smelled delicious from the baking cake.

Goose, duck, rooster, and turkey wandered over to the wonderful smell of the baking cake. They stood around the oven sniffing and smiling.

"Mmmm," said the goose.

"Mmmm," said the duck.

"Mmmm," said the rooster.

"Mmmm," said the turkey.

The little red hen took the cake out of the oven to cool. "Who will help me eat the cake?" asked the little red hen.

"I will!" said the goose.

"I will!" said the duck.

"I will!" said the rooster.

"I will!" said the turkey.

But the little red hen just shook her head and said, "All by myself I planted the wheat, I watered the wheat, I cut the wheat, and I took the wheat to the mill to be ground into flour. All by myself I mixed the batter, I set the oven, and I watched the cake so it wouldn't burn. SO all by myself I'm going to eat it!" And she did!

Storytelling About Plants

Children will enjoy rhymes and tales about plants and trees.

Little Tiny Petals

Materials: flannelboard, fabric circle, fabric petals

Directions: Recite this rhyme, letting the children take turns placing a number of petals around the circle to make a flower. Let the rest of the children count the petals together.

Little tiny petals pretty as can be,
How many petals do we see?
Little tiny petals growing all around,
How many petals can be found?

Sometimes I Wish

Materials: flannelboard, two child cutouts (use one child cutout for the mother; pattern page 50), tiny fabric seed, fabric tree

Directions: Use fabric paint to add details to the cutouts. Let the children take turns "planting" the seed on the flannelboard and transforming it into a tree.

Sometimes I wish I were a seed,
To plant into the ground,
And when my mommy looked for me,
She'd think I'm not around.

I'd grow some roots and one long trunk,
To make myself real tall,
And when my mommy looked
   for me,
She'd not see me at all!

I'd grow some leaves
   and branches too,
To make food in sunlight,
And when my mommy
   looked for me,
She'd see a tree with
   height.

But then I'd wish I were a child,
To sing and dance and hum,
And when my mommy looked for me,
She'd call me and I'd come!

Planting Flowers in a Row

Materials: flannelboard, fabric circles, fabric petals, green fabric strips for stems, tiny fabric leaves

Directions: As you recite this rhyme, begin placing flowers in a row on the flannelboard. Provide an empty flower seed package, a gardening hand tool, and a watering can for children to use in simulating the planting, weeding, and watering of the flowers.

Planting flowers in a row,
In a row, in a row,
Planting flowers in a row,
Sow, sow, sow.

Weeding flowers in a row,
In a row, in a row,
Weeding flowers in a row,
Hoe, hoe, hoe.

Watering flowers in a row,
In a row, in a row,
Watering flowers in a row,
Grow, grow, grow!

Picking flowers in a row,
In a row, in a row,
Picking flowers in a row,
No! No! No!

I Have a Little Plant

Materials: flannelboard, fabric circle, fabric petals, green fabric strip for stem, long strips of green fabric for vines, tiny fabric leaves

Directions: Recite this rhyme, letting the children take turns creating a flower that has leaves and long vines.

I have a little plant,
With vines that like to crawl,
Right out in the sunshine,
And all along the wall.

I wish my plant could talk,
And sing with me and play,
So I could have a friend,
Beside me every day!

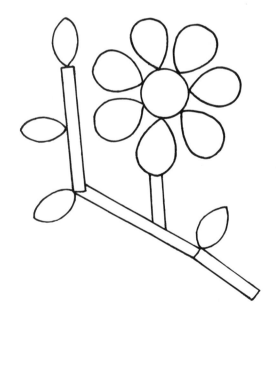

Storytelling About Our World

Here are story rhymes and songs about stars, Earth, the moon, and the sun.

"Earth Is Spinning" Song

Materials: flannelboard; Earth, moon, and star cutouts (pattern page 62); sun cutout (pattern page 56)

Directions: Use fabric paint to add details to the cutouts. Teach the children this story song sung to the tune of "Are You Sleeping?" Talk about day and night. Help the children understand that the stars are out even in the daytime. Tell the children that it takes one day for Earth to complete one spin. Let the children take turns placing the cutouts on the flannelboard.

Earth is spinning,
Earth is spinning,
Round and round,
Round and round,
Twinkling stars hide their light,
Sun is shining so bright,
Moon is near,
Day is here.

Earth is spinning,
Earth is spinning,
Round and round,
Round and round,
Twinkling stars are so bright,
Sun is hiding its light,
Moon is near,
Night is here.

I See the Stars

Materials: flannelboard, star cutouts (pattern page 62)

Directions: Make several star cutouts. Talk about wishes. Let the children share some of their wishes. Teach the children this rhyme. While the children recite it, let one child place a number of stars on the flannelboard. Have the rest of the children count the stars.

Twinkle, twinkle stars at night,
Make a wish on a twinkling light!
I see stars and stars see me,
How many bright stars can *you* see?

Up in the Sky

Directions: Use fabric paint to add details to the cutouts. Add yarn hair and fabric clothing on the child cutouts. Talk about the sun giving us heat and light. Tell the children that sunlight helps plants and animals grow and that it allows us to see color. Let the children take turns manipulating the cutouts as you tell this story rhyme.

Up in the sky far far away,
The sun shines its light,
On the earth all day.

Up in the sky far far away,
The sun sends out heat,
On the earth all day.

Up in the sky far far away,
The sun helps things grow,
On the earth all day.

Up in the sky far far away,
The sun makes us smile,
On the earth all day.

Ten Little Stars

Directions: Use fabric paint to add details to the cutouts. Let the children take turns manipulating the cutouts as you tell this story rhyme.

Ten little stars twinkling in the sky,
One disappeared,
When the sun reappeared.

Nine little stars twinkling in the sky,
One disappeared,
When the sun reappeared.

Eight little stars twinkling in the sky,
(*and so on*)

One little star twinkling in the sky,
It disappeared,
When the sun
reappeared.

Ten little stars
twinkling in
the sky,
All reappeared,
When the sun disappeared!

Storytelling About Food

Story rhymes about fruits, vegetables, and healthy eating are fun!

juicy and great to bring along.

Meats, beans, and nuts help you grow up big and strong.

Milk and dairy products help to make your teeth shine bright.

Extras is the junk food group; it's the last stuff you should bite.

Six food groups for breakfast, lunch, and dinner, Eat them in balanced meals, and you'll always be a winner!

Food Groups, Food Groups

Materials: flannelboard, food cutouts (pattern pages 54–55, 61), child cutouts (pattern page 50), mini-sentence strips, self-sticking Velcro

Directions: Use fabric paint to add details to the cutouts. Add yarn hair and fabric clothing to the child cutouts. Write the name of each food group on a separate sentence strip. Attach a "hooks" piece of self-sticking Velcro to the back of each strip. Place the strips on the flannelboard. Let the children take turns sorting the food cutouts into the six food groups.

Food groups, food groups,
Make a healthy me!
Food groups, food groups,
What can they be?

Breads and grains give you energy to run and jump and play.

Vegetables help you look your best, so eat them every day.

Fruits are sweet and

Twelve Fresh Eggs

Materials: flannelboard, 12 egg cutouts (pattern page 61)

Directions: Let the children take turns removing an egg from the dozen eggs lined up on the flannelboard.

Twelve fresh eggs,
From the grocery store,
One cracked its shell,
And oozed on the floor!

Eleven fresh eggs, (*and so on*)

One fresh egg,
From the grocery store,
Just cracked its shell,
And oozed on the floor . . .
What a mess! (*shout*)

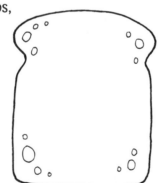

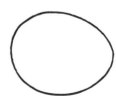

Going on a Picnic

Materials: flannelboard, food cutouts (pattern pages 54–55, 61, 63)

Directions: Let the children take turns placing the food cutouts in sequence on the flannelboard.

Going on a picnic,
What shall we take?
Apples and cheese,
Chocolate cake.

Going on a picnic,
What shall we bring?
Carrots and grapes,
Candy on string.

Going on a picnic,
What shall we eat?
Turkey and bread,
Bananas sweet!

Going on a picnic,
What shall we do?
Eat, eat, and eat,
Rest when we're through!

I Have a Shiny Apple

Materials: flannelboard, apple cutout (pattern page 54), several fabric apple slices

Directions: Let the children take turns placing a certain number of apple slices on the flannelboard. Let the rest of the children count the slices.

I have a shiny apple,
To share with you and me.
Watch me slice my apple,
As thin as thin can be.

alligator (8, 33)

monkey (8)

child (9, 11, 12, 15, 19, 21, 22, 25, 31, 34, 35, 41, 44, 47, 48)

cow (41)

Teacher: Enlarge or reduce copies of the patterns to vary the sizes of the cutouts. Laminate or cover them with clear self-sticking paper for sturdiness. Use them as cutouts or as templates for tracing on felt or other fabrics.

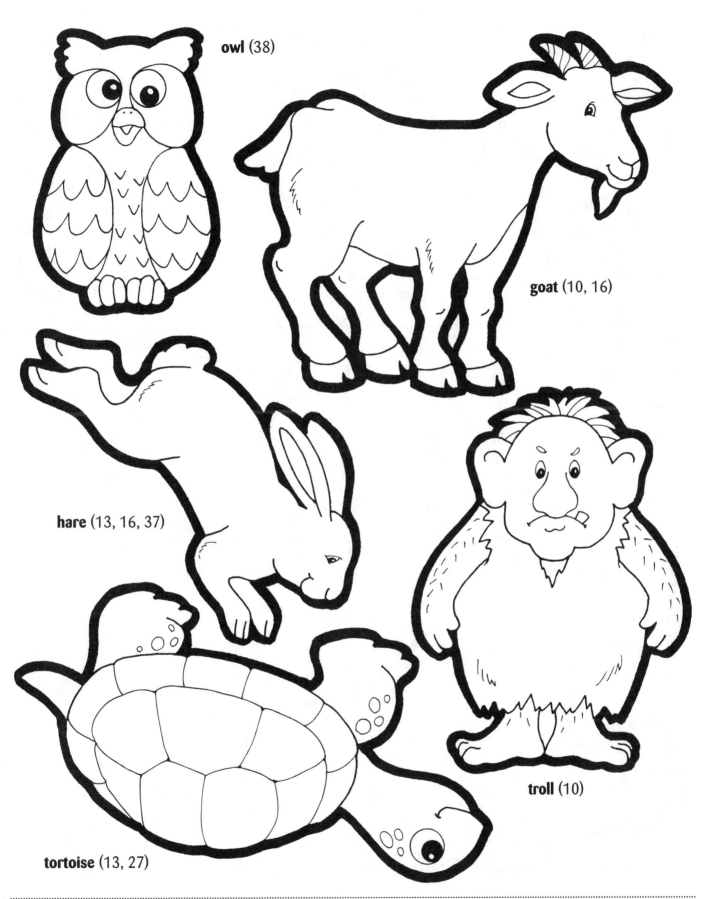

owl (38)

goat (10, 16)

hare (13, 16, 37)

troll (10)

tortoise (13, 27)

bears (11, 16, 21, 36, 37)

dog (13, 25, 36, 37)

chairs (11)

Teacher: Enlarge or reduce copies of the patterns to vary the sizes of the cutouts. Laminate or cover them with clear self-sticking paper for sturdiness. Use them as cutouts or as templates for tracing on felt or other fabrics.

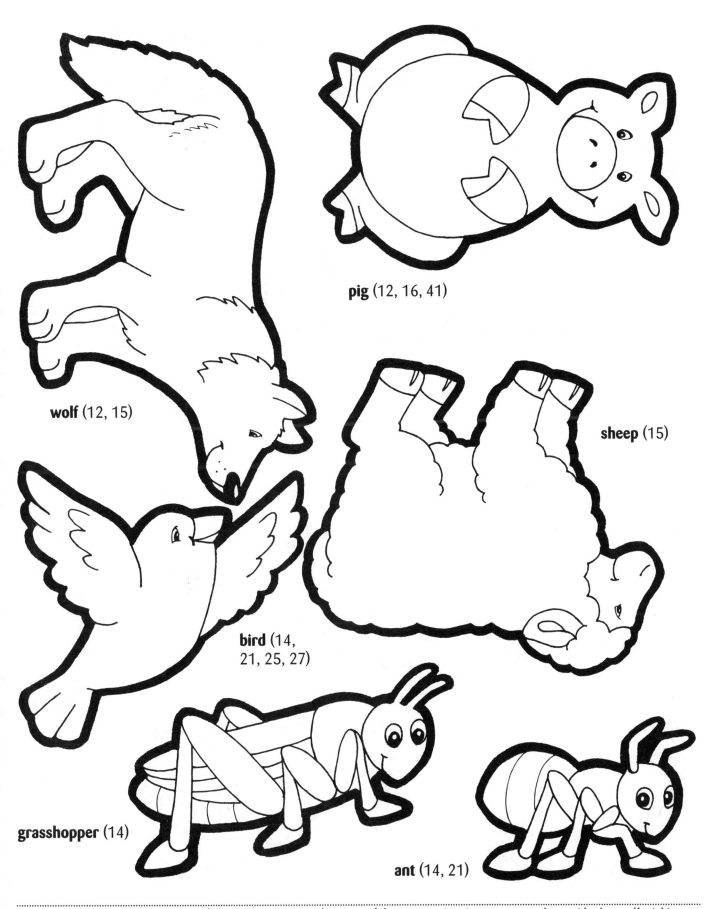

pig (12, 16, 41)

wolf (12, 15)

sheep (15)

bird (14, 21, 25, 27)

grasshopper (14)

ant (14, 21)

grapes (15, 31, 48, 49)

leaf (17, 18, 40)

pumpkin (18, 48)

fox (15, 37)

apple (9, 16, 17, 31, 38, 48, 49)

Teacher: Enlarge or reduce copies of the patterns to vary the sizes of the cutouts. Laminate or cover them with clear self-sticking paper for sturdiness. Use them as cutouts or as templates for tracing on felt or other fabrics.

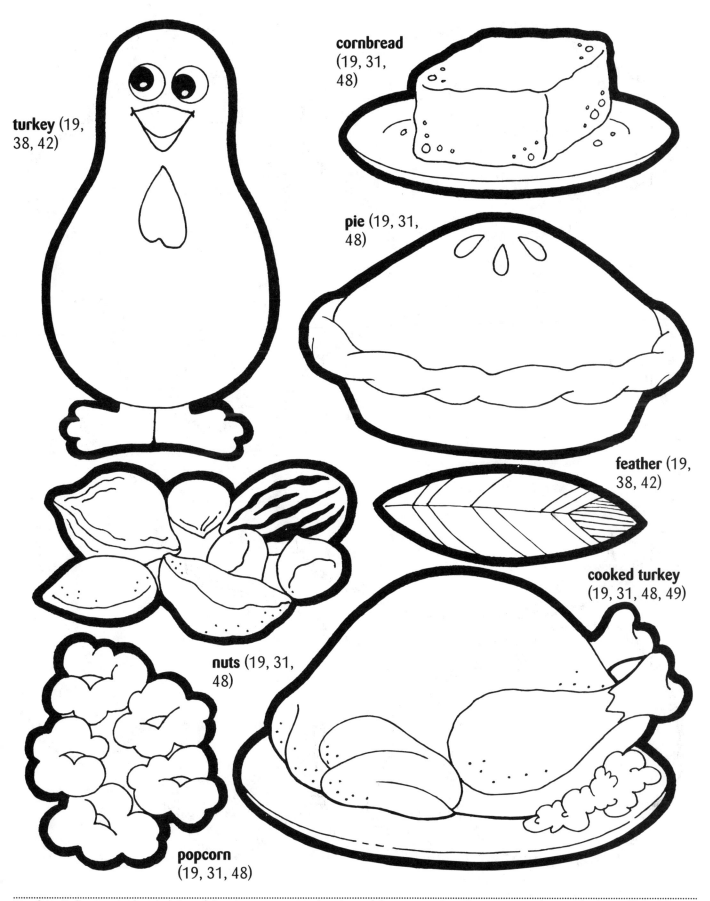

turkey (19, 38, 42)

cornbread (19, 31, 48)

pie (19, 31, 48)

feather (19, 38, 42)

cooked turkey (19, 31, 48, 49)

nuts (19, 31, 48)

popcorn (19, 31, 48)

Teacher: Enlarge or reduce copies of the patterns to vary the sizes of the cutouts. Laminate or cover them with clear self-sticking paper for sturdiness. Use them as cutouts or as templates for tracing on felt or other fabrics.

snowman (20, 23)

sun (20, 23, 26, 27, 46, 47)

snowflake (21)

top hat (20, 23)

horse (41)

Teacher: Enlarge or reduce copies of the patterns to vary the sizes of the cutouts. Laminate or cover them with clear self-sticking paper for sturdiness. Use them as cutouts or as templates for tracing on felt or other fabrics.

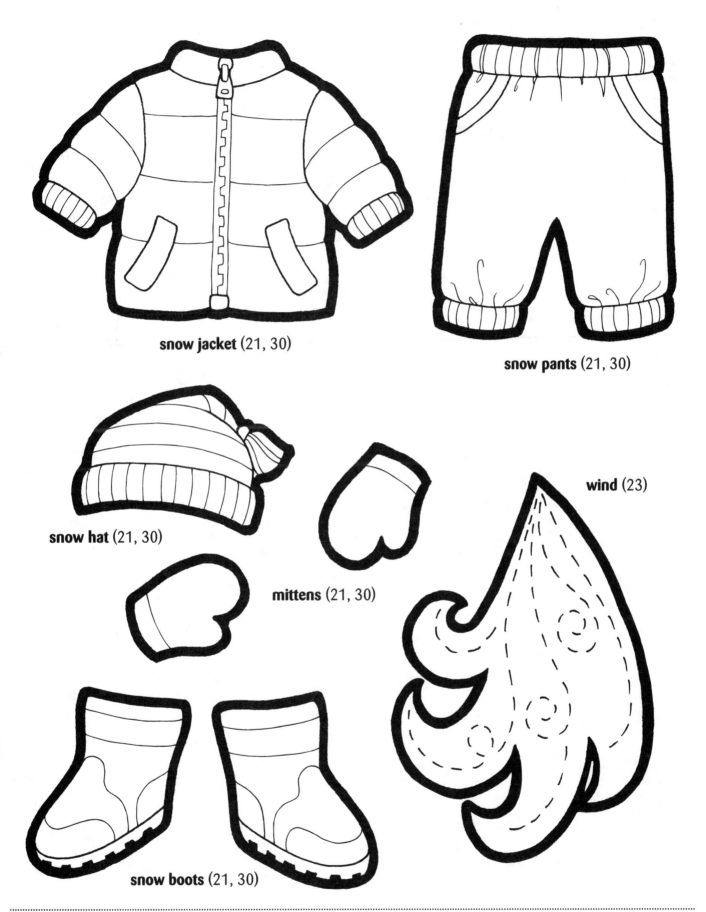

snow jacket (21, 30)

snow pants (21, 30)

snow hat (21, 30)

mittens (21, 30)

wind (23)

snow boots (21, 30)

heart (33, 40)

flower (24, 47)

bee (25, 28)

beehive (28)

bunny (25)

Teacher: Enlarge or reduce copies of the patterns to vary the sizes of the cutouts. Laminate or cover them with clear self-sticking paper for sturdiness. Use them as cutouts or as templates for tracing on felt or other fabrics.

raindrop (26, 27)

umbrella (26)

duck (26, 27, 38, 41, 42)

rooster (38, 42)

spider (27)

Teacher: Enlarge or reduce copies of the patterns to vary the sizes of the cutouts. Laminate or cover them with clear self-sticking paper for sturdiness. Use them as cutouts or as templates for tracing on felt or other fabrics.

59

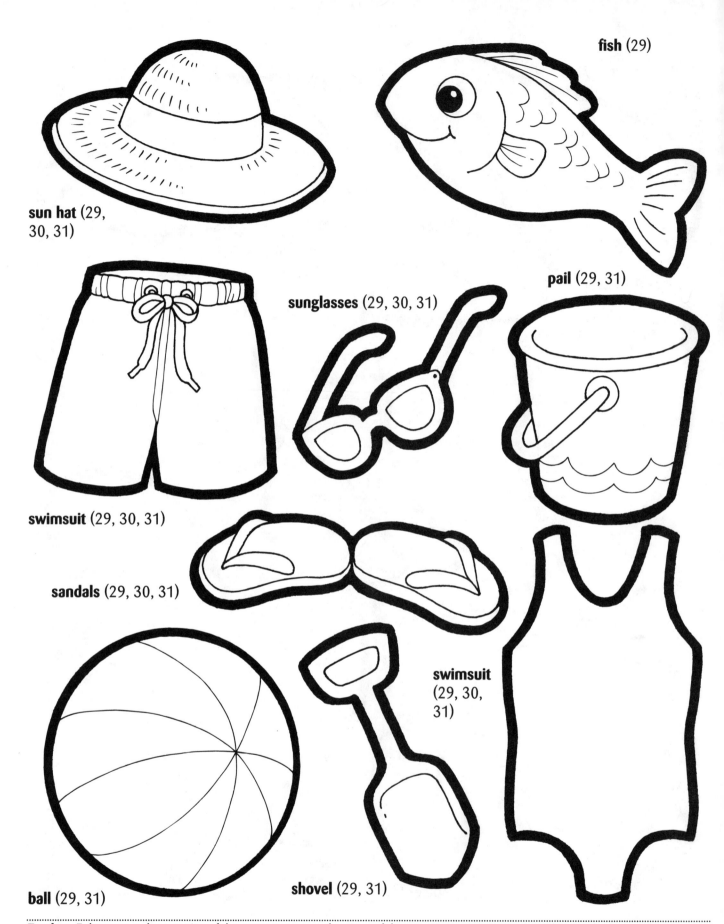

fish (29)

sun hat (29, 30, 31)

pail (29, 31)

sunglasses (29, 30, 31)

swimsuit (29, 30, 31)

sandals (29, 30, 31)

swimsuit (29, 30, 31)

ball (29, 31)

shovel (29, 31)

Teacher: Enlarge or reduce copies of the patterns to vary the sizes of the cutouts. Laminate or cover them with clear self-sticking paper for sturdiness. Use them as cutouts or as templates for tracing on felt or other fabrics.

frosting (32, 48)

flour (32, 42, 48)

salt (32, 48)

cake pan (32, 42)

candle (22, 32)

egg (32, 42, 48)

sugar (32, 42, 48)

bowl (32, 42)

flame (22, 32)

milk (32, 42, 48)

cake (32, 42, 49)

Teacher: Enlarge or reduce copies of the patterns to vary the sizes of the cutouts. Laminate or cover them with clear self-sticking paper for sturdiness. Use them as cutouts or as templates for tracing on felt or other fabrics.

Earth (46)

moon (36, 46)

dish (36)

fiddle (36)

cat (36, 37)

spoon (36)

star (46, 47)

Teacher: Enlarge or reduce copies of the patterns to vary the sizes of the cutouts. Laminate or cover them with clear self-sticking paper for sturdiness. Use them as cutouts or as templates for tracing on felt or other fabrics.

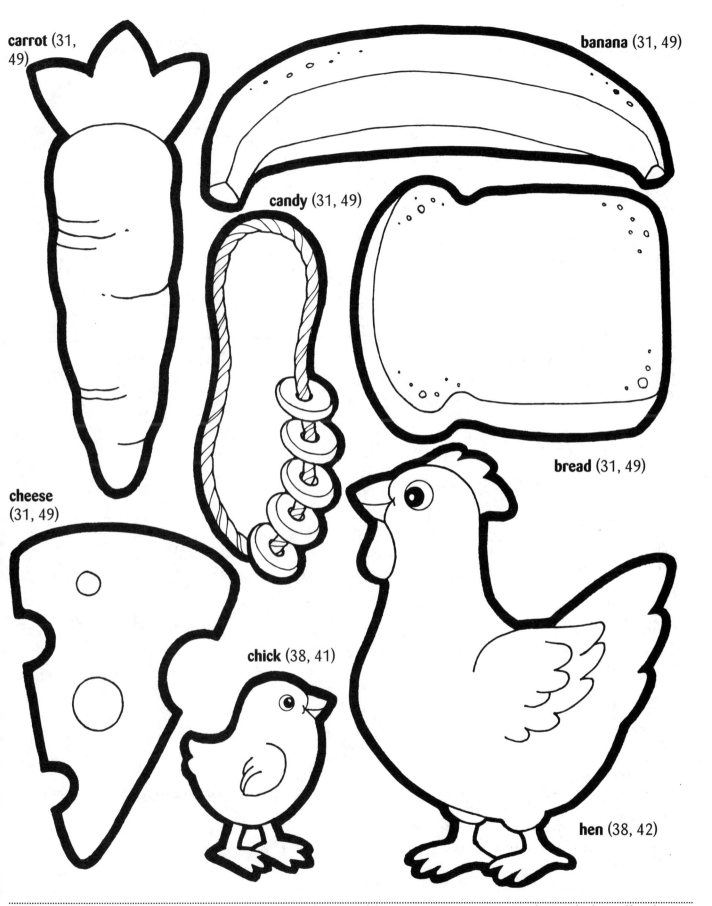

carrot (31, 49)

banana (31, 49)

candy (31, 49)

bread (31, 49)

cheese (31, 49)

chick (38, 41)

hen (38, 42)

Teacher: Enlarge or reduce copies of the patterns to vary the sizes of the cutouts. Laminate or cover them with clear self-sticking paper for sturdiness. Use them as cutouts or as templates for tracing on felt or other fabrics.

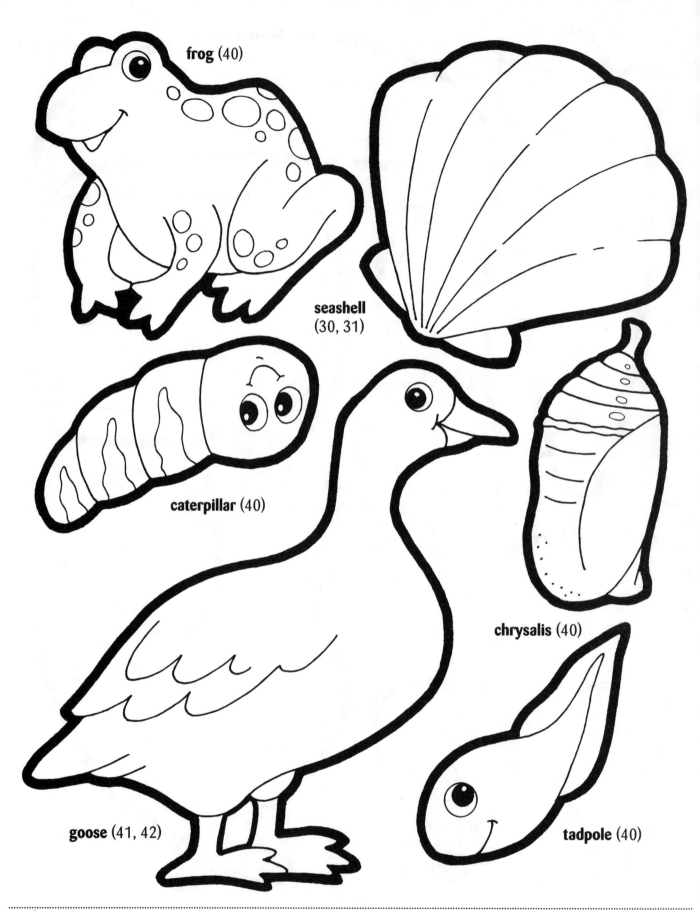

frog (40)

seashell (30, 31)

caterpillar (40)

chrysalis (40)

goose (41, 42)

tadpole (40)

Teacher: Enlarge or reduce copies of the patterns to vary the sizes of the cutouts. Laminate or cover them with clear self-sticking paper for sturdiness. Use them as cutouts or as templates for tracing on felt or other fabrics.